"May I have a pet?"
"You bet!"

"Where will we get my pet?"

"At the pound."

5

Ten pounds of pet!

Pet to the vet.

"All set."

Wet pet.

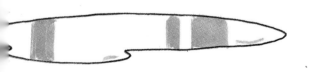

Wet Pat!

"Have you met my pet?"
"Not yet."

"Your pet has your hat, Pat!"

"See your pet bat your hat!"

"Stop that!"

"Play with this stick."

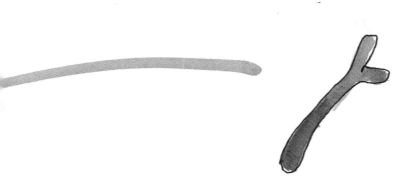

"He learned his first trick!"

A pat for the pet.

A pet for Pat.
That's that!

WORDS

		that
	learned	that's
a	met	ten
all	may	the
at	my	this
bat	not	to
bet	of	trick
first	Pat	vet
for	pet	we
get	play	wet
has	pound	where
hat	pounds	will
have	see	with
he	set	yet
his	stick	you
I	stop	your

About the Author

A *Pet for Pat* is the second book by **Pegeen Snow** to be published by Childrens Press. In addition, her short stories and light verse have appeared in a variety of publications. A native of Eau Claire, Wisconsin, Ms. Snow's non-writing interests include "noodling at the piano, de-fleaing the cats, and trying to fix up an obstinate house."

About the Artist

Tom Dunnington divides his time between book illustration and wildlife painting. He has done many books for Childrens Press, as well as working on textbooks, and is a regular contributor to "Highlights for Children." Tom lives in Oak Park, Illinois.